FOUR SWANS

FOUR SWANS

poems

Greg Pape

Lynx House Press
Spokane, Washington

ACKNOWLEDGMENTS

Thanks to the editors of the following publications in which these poems first appeared:

Field: "Red Moon"
Gulf Stream Magazine: "Driving Through"
High Horse: "Some Guardian Spirit"
Lake Effect: "Spring Storm"
Long Journey: Contemporary Northwest Poets: "Four Swans"
Luna: "The Living Hair of Travelers"
Northwest Review: "Cemetery in Kentucky" and "Etheridge"
Poems Across the Big Sky: An Anthology of Montana Poets: "Elegy for Jim
    Welch"
Poets of the American West: "Lower Yellowstone Falls" and "View of the
    Bitterroot"
Sonora Review: "Likeness"
Sugar House Review: "Big Lost River Breakdown"
The Florida Review: "Evening Landscape:
The Louisville Review: "Deer in the Garden," "Elegy for Big Red" and "That
    Space Inside Them"
Willow Springs: "Steps"

The following poems first appeared in the chapbook, *Animal Time*: "The Dipper in Winter," "Tracks & Traces," "If Wishes Were," "The Wooly Mammoths," "Lar & Deer" and "Dog"

Cover Art by Ken Bushe: *Swans at Pebble Beach*, Oil on canvas, 30 x 36" This and other fine paintings by Ken Bushe can be viewed online at www.kenbushe.co.uk.
Author Photo: Tammy Ramsey
Book Design: Christine Holbert

FIRST EDITION

ISBN 978-088924-127-2

Cataloging-in-Publication Data is available from the Library of Congress.

CONTENTS

I

Four Swans · 1

Under a Waxing Moon · 4

Some Guardian Spirit · 5

The Dipper in Winter · 6

Ice Fishing in a Snowstorm · 7

On the Road to Great Falls · 9

Birthday Bird Count · 11

Homage to Su Tung-p'o · 13

Tracks & Traces · 17

The Six Directions · 19

If Wishes Were · 20

The Wooly Mammoths · 21

II

Bitterroot Suite · 25

Spring Storm · 28

Saturday Morning · 29

Undersong · 30

Steps · 32

The Living Hair of Travelers · 34

Driving Through · 35

Likeness · 37

Elegy for Big Red · 38

Reading Montana · 41

Lunch in Lima · 43

The Spell of the Bitterroot · 44

Rain on the River · 46

III

Lower Yellowstone Falls · 49

Rattlesnake Bend · 50

Evening Landscape · 52

Notes for a Painting · 53

After the Fireworks · 54

Etheridge · 55

Elegy for Jim Welch · 56

Big Lost River Breakdown · 57

Red Moon · 61

Luminous Hour · 63

Where Sunlight Falls · 64

Lar & Deer · 65

IV

That Space Inside Them · 69

Deer in the Garden · 70

Harvest Home · 71

Praise · 72

View of the Bitterroot · 73

A Gold Star for Crumley · 74

Elegy for the Yangtze · 75

Dog · 76

Good Night Irene · 77

Irene · 79

Cemetery in Kentucky · 80

White Church in Wiborg · 82

Notes · 85

In memory of my mother, Irene Pape

I

FOUR SWANS

A northern harrier glides low over the tules.

A pair of mallards, their tail feathers
tipped up to the sun, feed in what's left
of the open water on Whistler Pond.

January. Four white tundra swans
stand at the edge of the ice.

Grace. Peace. Dignity. X.

X stretches her long gorgeous neck,
steps off the ice onto the water
and keeps walking.

When I spoke on the phone with my mother
in the hospital, someone was dying

in the background. I imagined hope
dripped from a pouch into a tube
into a vein. A moan

took off and scaled up into a scream.
I can't talk, my mother said, firmly,
and there at the margins of her voice

some hard anger pushed against terror.
Pain sat and watched.

Now I sit and watch the swan
walk on water. There must be

a shelf of ice just under the surface.

She lowers herself, and with a twitch
of her tail feathers, pushes off
and glides into the open water,

not like the setting out at the beginning
of a story, more like easing into

a new stillness, this white house of down
and feathers from which the ripples
move outward, signals from a beacon,

but at the same time appear
to move inward, drawn, repelled and drawn.

I see a boy drawn to the window
of the last house on Congress Street,
the small white adobe at the foot
of Tumamoc Hill in Tucson. He is

looking at the full moon
through bare branches of the Palo Verde tree,
imagining the body spread-eagle, caught

in flight by those branches
a dozen yards from the spot Joe Galindo's
motorcycle hit the wall at sixty.

To him Galindo is a story told by the neighbors,
a cautionary tale of speed and booze
and reckless disregard.

To him Galindo is a moonlit thought
tangled in the limbs among his own
confusions, a ghost among other ghosts,

only this one the closest, the one that holds sway
between the Palo Verde and the small cave
in the hillside where the plaster statue

of Saint Jude resides. Maybe X
I should name Saint Jude, patron saint of all the Xs.

She feeds on the pond bottom
with the mallards.

She works her black feet back and forth
in the bottom-mud stirring things up

then lowers her long neck in a bow
and dips her head into the water.

UNDER A WAXING MOON

Under a waxing moon cool rain fell for hours.
An owl dozed, ducks preened, the heron hunched low for hours.

Nothing could account for the way she moved.
He stared at the window streaked with rain remembering for hours.

The map torn, the route uncertain, tire flat,
bottle empty, they laughed, it seemed, for hours.

I don't care for flags, he said, or limousines, funeral homes,
headstones—sick of the news, he didn't care for hours.

A monk sat still as moonlight on a frozen lake
emptying his mind, counting his breaths for hours.

SOME GUARDIAN SPIRIT

Freezing fog, visibility maybe a hundred yards.
Frost builds up on the pine needles,
the yellow grass, the leafless cottonwoods
and apple trees. Voices of carpenters
and the sound of hammers, saws,
a compressor kicking on and off
in that other world somewhere across
the pasture. Not a bird or a squirrel or a horse
in sight. A rooster and a lone dog
send their voices out into the fog that seems
to be closing in, growing denser, a cloud
barge drifting down the valley spiriting us away.

Sometimes the smaller the world the better.
This windowsill is a true horizon.
In one of the rooms down this cloud hall
someone may be waiting for someone
to listen to a story that needs to be told.
Right here, in the wavy lines of the wood grain
there's a kind of far-off water sound
a hush of low tide, salt scent, footprints
in the sand, someone walking in the fog,
her black shoes in her hand, a little worn out
from all the worrying, the dull hours of work,
the gossip, the waiting, the news, the grief,
the anger, all of it, lulled now by the waves, coming
slowly back to herself, grateful for what she
can't hear or see, feeling close to something
she won't try to name, some guardian spirit
maybe, content just to be walking with her
in the fog like this.

THE DIPPER IN WINTER

Not Ursa Major whose outer edge
points at Polaris, our north star,
or the seven sisters of the Pleiades,
the six daughters of Atlas who shine
dark nights for the one who is lost,
but the little slate-black river bird
always rocking and bobbing
to an inner music at the edges
of ice, slick stone and cold water.
The one who flies low and goes
down under the surface to see
what the fish and the water spirits see,
down in the current where sun
and stars stream and smooth
the hard edges, regrets and fears,
all those many-colored flamingos
of time and desire asleep
in their watery feathers. Cheers,
she says, and bobs and dips and
disappears.

ICE FISHING IN A SNOWSTORM

Sitting on an overturned bucket,
back to the blowing snow,
watching my line through a hole
in the ice, I think of Liu Tsung-yuan's
poem, River Snow—

From a thousand hills, birds have vanished,
on ten thousand paths, human traces gone.
Lone boat, an old man in straw hat and cloak,
fishing alone in the cold river snow.

So much resonates from all those o's.
The boat and the old man float on the water
apart from *the endless, oblivious business*
of the world. The ice
is eighteen inches thick and yet we float
in the blowing snow, in a fine mindless
concentration, but also mindful of the snow,
the wind, and what they can do.

I have to skim the ice often
with a ladle so I can peer down into the hole
where trout swim among the lines
that go down almost to the bottom,
where cutthroat, rainbow, and brook trout—
say red is on his side like apples in a fog
(that voice like a shot
of whiskey in a snowstorm)—
swim among the lines.

Like the old man, alone, I say we
because Liu Tsung-yuan, Tu Fu, and Hugo
look over my shoulder into the little lake
of clear water I opened with the auger, water

that wants to ice-over, wants to freeze-up
more solidly than ever. Ice in an old hole
will dull or break the blades of the auger.
You have to cut a new hole.
You have to sit in the snow and wait.

ON THE ROAD TO GREAT FALLS

The bighorn sheep browsing along the edge
of Highway 200, where the forest ends
at the barrow pit, seem to ignore me as I pass by
in my truck at 70 mph. That big full-curl ram,
with his dirty buff wool and yellow eye
looks like a creature from another time, mythic
and real at once. He is Aries, the first sign
of the zodiac, who ushers in the Spring.
Two steps away from an explosion of blood
on the highway, and yet he seems to hold
the old world in place with his imperturbable
grace. What do I share with this creature
besides the air we breathe and that brief space
above the Blackfoot River where both our hearts
beat calmly as we passed within a few feet
of each other, two worlds that could have collided
but didn't? Now we're both breathing the cold
Spring air, in present tense, in the same world
we all depend on, but look at and respond to
so differently. I slow to 35 as I pass through
Lincoln, that small unpretentious mountain town
made briefly and sadly famous by Ted Kaczynski,
a whiz with figures, but a complete failure
at human relations. Soon I will cross the Continental
Divide at Rogers Pass, where the coldest temperature
in the lower forty-eight states was recorded, -73°.
Today snow comes down to the edge of the road,
and there's ice at the top of the pass. Today,
as usual, someone somewhere is constructing
a bomb. You'd think one of the world's foremost
philosophies could be summed up by the proposition,
explosions solve problems. From this vantage point
high on the Divide the land begins to open.
It is like the yellow eye of that ram. It sees

right through you. It's as if you were as clear
as the water in the Dearborn River, which is
headed the same way you are, past the bouquets
of white crosses at Bowman's Corner, past
Sun River, and on to Great Falls.

BIRTHDAY BIRD COUNT

Fifty-six ducks, mostly mallards, swimming in what's left
of the open water, ice closing in.

Many ravens, hard to count, two, maybe three-dozen
milling around in hoar-frosted pines, a dead deer nearby.

One long-eared owl on a low branch stares, holds me
a moment like a vole in its big gold eyes.

One bald eagle headed upriver stroking and gliding,
reading the water's scroll of riffles, runs, and pools.

One killdeer limping off through the air leading me away
out of habit from the nest she won't make for months.

One dipper steps off a rock and goes under like a bobber.

Near the rusted turquoise roof of an old car embedded
in the riverbank, ice feathers of some dream bird poised
above the water.

On the far side of the river twenty-three more mallards
feeding among stones, looking themselves like stones.

Add to these ten thousand sanderlings lighting the air
near Mono Lake, east of the Sierra,

the sandhill cranes purling in the hayfields outside
Last Chance, Idaho,

the magnificent frigate birds and black and white skimmers
working the water off Flamingo,

and the flamingos of Hialeah, the spoonbills of Buck Key,
the pelicans of Captiva, my father's blackbird, my mother's
cardinal, clouds of sea birds falling like hail on the waters off Isla
Piedra,

and this lone blue heron painting the dusk with slow wing strokes
almost touching the tops of the pines,
in no hurry to disappear.

HOMAGE TO SU TUNG-P'O

A strong offshore wind feathers the tips of big waves rising against a gray sky, breaking over the black rocks of the jetty. I sit watching from the beach, my little brother beside me in the wind. Two surfers take off on the same huge wave. They angle across the face, away from the rocks, their boards almost touching. They stand side by side, moving with the water, and, as they make the drop, seem to steady each other with their arms. The wave curls and breaks. They disappear in surging whitewater. I turn and there is no one beside me. My little brother is gone. I must find him, in the dream I wake from, for a moment unsure where I am—

Outside this dark room does surf pound in the distance? Does early traffic rush between the lights of Redondo, Fresno, Tuscaloosa, Louisville, Miami, Tucson?

Now, through the window at dawn, I see a light snow is falling. Home in the Bitterroot. Self and place, a loose weave, a falling fabric, snow.

Tracks of deer, coyote, and fox
tell a cold story of night
in huge calligraphy across the snowy hills.

In 1079 Su Shih was arrested on charges of "slandering the emperor" in his poems. He was imprisoned and subjected to fierce interrogation.

He wrote from prison: "The officials treat me with increasing harshness, and I doubt that I can stand it much longer. If I die in prison, I will have no chance to say goodbye to Tzu-yu (his brother), and therefore I wrote these two poems and gave them to the warden, Liang Hsu, to deliver to him."

Here is the first of the two poems:

Under the heaven of our holy ruler, all things turn to spring,
But I in dark ignorance have destroyed myself.
Before my hundred years are past, I'm called to settle up;

My leaderless family, ten mouths, must be your worry now.
Bury me anywhere on the green hills
And another year in night rain grieve for me alone.
Let us be brothers in lives and lives to come,
Mending then the bonds that this world breaks.

After a confinement of 130 days in prison Su was released and assigned a minor post with the water bureau in the region of Huang-Chou north of the Yangtze River. He was banished to live in exile, but greatly relieved to be released from prison alive, he wrote the following poem:

A hundred days, free to go, and it's almost spring;
For the years left, pleasure will be my chief concern.
Out the gate, I stop to piss, wind blows my face;
Our galloping horses race along as magpies cheer.
I face the wine cup and it's all a dream,
Pick up a poem brush, already inspired.
Why try to fix blame for trouble past?
Years now I've stolen posts I never should have had.

True to the spirit of his poem Su strove to be a happy exile. In a letter to his friend Chin Kuan he reveals his cheerful outlook: "I figure I still have enough money left (food was plentiful and cheap) to last us a year or more, and after that we'll think of something else. Running water digs a ditch—"

In Huang-Chou, after two years of increasing poverty, with the intercession of his friend Ma Cheng Ch'ing, he was given the use of some poor land he named Tung-p'o or Eastern Slope. He cleared the land of rubble and weeds, tilled, and planted wheat, rice, mulberries, bamboo and pine, and turned that "several tens of mou," maybe five acres, once an army camp, into a flourishing farm.

Working the land and seeing it come back to life so moved him that he took Tung-p'o as his hao or literary name.

Reading his poems, in the Burton Watson translations, I find in Su Tung-p'o a friend across time.

The moon waxes and wanes, and yet in the end it's the same moon.

His dream of the Taoist immortal disguised as a black-and-white crane flying above the river is my dream. His pleasure in words—finding them, arranging them in clear sentences, satisfying lines—is my pleasure.

Man on a fast horse, thin robe flying, sketched in one stroke.

His hope and joy in working the land
I share:

Last night clouds came from hills to the south;
Rain soaked the ground a plowshare deep.
Rivulets found the channel again,
Knowing I'd chopped back the weeds.
In the mud a few old roots of cress
Still alive from a year ago.
If white buds will open again,
When spring doves come I'll make a stew!

His love for his brother Tzu-yu
echoes here in my brother's broad smile
as I find him again walking up the beach in the wind,
at the front door late at night in the rain,
in a raft on the river, a canoe on the lake,
at the kitchen table drinking a glass of wine.

Ditch full of leaves and snow, it's the middle of winter in Montana. The sun reappears after many gray days. My boots shuffle through two inches of glinting surface snow and crunch through frozen layers beneath, as I walk to my study in the back woods at Eagles Point, a place I imagine like the small house Su built in 1082 at Eastern Slope. It's slow walking, good for stopping and looking around.

A hundred finches in the hawthorn thicket
celebrate the sun.

Wind is somewhere else, on the other side of the mountains.
The rooster can't stop crowing.

I think of my brother working late in his shop, kick the snow from my boots,
and open the door to South Hall to visit the good spirit, Su Tung-p'o.

Sweep the floor, burn incense, close the door to sleep;
A mat marked like water, curtains like mist.
I dream a guest comes, wake wondering where I am,
Prop open the west window on waves that meet the sky.

TRACKS & TRACES

Slabs of ice covered with snow
and the tracks of an otter who came ashore
and bounded along a curved path
for fifty feet and lowered its tail
and slid back into the water.
It must be fun to be an otter.
Farther on, tracks of a couple dozen geese
who'd had a meeting on the ice.
It must have been cordial, no one
stepped in another's tracks, and it must
have ended suddenly with them all
lifting at once into the air.
Wouldn't that be something, to bend
your knees, to raise your arms
and spread your feathers and pull them
down and push off your webbed feet
and stretch out your long neck
and lift off into the air above the river
with a bunch of friends honking and barking
and lining up in a pattern that made sense
to everyone and seemed to ennoble the air?
Well, watch out for your lost brother
down there in the tules, calling and calling,
over here over here. His love is tender
and violent and hard to explain.
Brother goose, sister otter forgive us our ways.
We'll all sleep together, as T'ao Ch'ien said,
a bent arm on the pillow, keeping emptiness whole.

I go on walking, glancing down to see the path,
then up into the trees to see the trees, owls
maybe, great-horned, long-eared, sawhet,
woodpeckers, hairy, downy, pileated,
the brown creeper, the snipe, or porcupines,

those shy four-footed cacti of the north woods
who gnaw the bark and sweet cambium
of the young pines and climb higher
than the owls roost to roll up into a ball
of quills and sleep away the cold
like that old Buddhist monk called Bird's Nest
because he liked to sleep and meditate in the trees.
When I see one I bow backwards and gaze awhile
in porcupine time. Then I walk on, step over
a fallen branch, a rock. I walk until the path
fades and my steps find their way to a huge
uprooted Ponderosa pine wind tore loose
and lay down, leaving a cleft, a hole I step
down into, roots and rootlets still holding,
dangling in constellations, the rounded river stones
they clung to when the big wind came down
through Kootenai Canyon—a time of violence
become a place of shelter, part of the story
that houses us all.

THE SIX DIRECTIONS

The road out to the road is covered with snow
and lined with snow banks three feet deep.
My son stops to pose and smile, his arm
around a blue sled. The dog, who loved
the snow, walks with a limp in the cool shadows, wagging her tail.

Out the basement window I can look east
under the deck and see a chokecherry, apple,
and many cottonwood trees, today, all leafless, all gray.

And there is a wall of books, a bank of hours
spent in solitude with others, wandering;
The Land of Ulro, Far Tortuga, and side by side;
The Odyssey, Things Fall Apart, Name Your Baby.

Through the south window, where a fly
is throwing itself against a glass sky, I see
two far-off ponderosa pines, remnants
of a forest, a line of trailers, houses, barns,
and farther, patches of snow in old clear-cuts sixty miles south.

On the floor above, the kitchen, where the boys
are eating pancakes, and above them a bedroom
where the sheets are still warm, then a roof, a sky.

On the floor, a pair of feet on a rug riding a great wave
of upper belt rock and basin fill overlapping the batholith.

IF WISHES WERE

You could walk up any creek or canyon
in the Bitterroot watershed, One Horse, Sweeney,
Larry, Bass, Brooks, McCalla, Kootenai,
Big, Sweathouse, Bear, Fred Burr, Blodgett,
Sawtooth or Roaring Lion, and sit down,
feeling a little dizzy maybe, like the nuthatch
clinging upside down on the bark of a pine, and
make a wish.

Before long you might find yourself
wishing for something else. Remember
that old song, *Keep your eyes on the prize,*
and the line about the only chains we need
are the chains of these hands holding us together.
Somewhere over the rainbow there's a pot
of lottery tickets. I know the chances
are slim, one page in a ream, or worse, and the sky
is full of what we like to call stars, and if wishes were

horses, or a herd of confused elk down from deep snow
in the mountains, standing at the edge of the highway
watching us watch them as we speed by—maybe we
should just pull over, let things settle down, slow
to a slug's pace, and maybe they will cross over
to the river as if we hadn't fenced it off, as if
the highway meant them no harm. See the way
they seem to turn the pasture into an open prairie,
and every step they take has built-in dignity and grace.
Hold up. Here they come. Hold on.

THE WOOLY MAMMOTHS

What happened to the wooly mammoths?
We ate them, and they became us?
We had thought that early hunters,
after the invention of the atlatl and lethal
Clovis spear-point, killed off the wooly mammoths,
hunted them into extinction, along
with the saber-tooth tigers. Even the giant
armadillos could have succumbed
to the hunter's spear and cunning.
Isn't it a wonder the wooly mammoth
is much beloved among humans
who have never seen one except
in artist's recreations and bones
wired together in museums?
Those great aunts and uncles of the elephants
with their marvelous tusks and hilly demeanors
still roam the plains and vast interiors
of human dreamscapes. Now,
from fragments found in dry riverbeds
and lines of interstellar dust in the melting
glaciers, we've pieced together
a new theory of the mammoth's extinction.
It wasn't our spears but meteors laced
with minute diamonds unlike any jewels
of earth that rained from space
and set the land on fire.
If we have a picture, if we can smell
the earth, if we know hunger, if fire
has warmed us, if wind has cooled us,
if we have listened to water
and considered starlight, we can honor
the mammoths still roaming inside us,
we can make a story like a bowl from shards.

II

BITTERROOT SUITE

Because the whole is part, there's not a whole
anywhere, that is not part . . .
The sparrow stirs,
the universe moves slightly.

—Shinkichi Takahashi

Along the edge of the river three duck feathers
light and downy, curved upward and held
against stones like boats run aground
in green algae shallows.

Black leaves half submerged,
their veined structures, their brilliant stories
dissolving, turning to mud,
getting ready to live again as something else.

.

A foot higher than last week
the river has sunk the three duck feathers
that looked like proud boats run aground.
Now they are sodden wrecks awash in the waves.

A cold spring wind stings my cheeks.
Snow flurries drift like smoke
over the mountains. I have to write
with my gloves on, sitting here
on the trunk of a fallen cottonwood,
its roots jutting out over the water.
An arm's length away there's a pile
of scat six inches deep, from bleached white
to fresh black—this root perch, my seat of meditation,
must be the marmot's outhouse.

·

All along the trail five-petal buttercups
hold melting snow crystals. Sun
breaking through clouds turns crystals
to water beads. Bend down to look
more closely, see the weather changing
in each small globe. Wind, light breeze,

stillness. High up above the river
two red-tailed hawks soar, far
black silhouettes against changing shades
of gray, flashing their colors
in long shafts of sunlight.
Swallows dart among snowflakes
and raindrops, feeding on the hatch.
Trout rise in the bubble line
below the cutbank. Voices of flickers,
killdeers, red-winged blackbirds, the high
shrill cries of hawks weave patterns
through the air. Here comes a woman
with a black lab on a leash, a purple
sweater tied around her waist.
She stops. The dog stops.
She gazes up over the treetops.
The dog follows her gaze.

·

Sun sparks and glitters on the river.
Seeds drift and ride currents
in updrafts and swirls, the cottony fibers
of their flying skirts catching the light
then vanishing into the big mind of the air.

Melting snow crystals make a ticking sound.
Shreds of cottonwood bark move like ribbons,

like blond hair in the ground breeze
blowing over the gravel bar.

In a blue pontoon boat a fisherman
drifts by, his line ahead of him in the water.
He nods, mends his line. A pair of geese
come barking upstream just overhead.
I hear the swish and whistle of their wings
as they bank, rise, turn west and disappear
in the dark backdrop of the Bitterroots.
Hip deep in the river now,
I feel the cold pull of current against my legs,
feel its hold and flow in my bones.

SPRING STORM

A pause in the light,
in birdsong.
The weightless end
of an hour falls.
A storm blows in
over the Bitterroots.
Wind pushes flurries
into the silvery valley light,
finding voice in bare limbs
of cottonwoods, already budding,
waving, humming low notes
under the green brushes of pines.
All down the valley
doors are closing.
All down the valley horses
are turning east
as a backlit curtain of snow
closes on the southern vista.
One gray and black
bearpaw appaloosa
on a fenced half acre
runs tight circles in the dirt,
throwing its head, shaking its mane,
rocking forward, cocking
its spotted haunches,
kicking the teeth out of the wind.

SATURDAY MORNING

A house full of boys,
wild boys growling like dogs,
galloping across the living room floor,

bounding on the couch with gorilla grace,
blasting each other with pillows
and sleeping bags. Blake said exuberance

is beauty, and I can see it, but
at some point they will have to be cautioned,
urged in the direction of restraint, and soon.

More and more I have come to love
the stillness of morning, the opening
of day like the turning of a page

in a story I can't stop writing.
All the wise teachers say include the difficulties
in the work, keep your practice going.

So I will begin now to simmer the bacon.
I will mix the batter, fill the glasses
with cold juice of apples, oranges.

I will warm the maple syrup the way
my grandmother did, and if I raise
my voice it will not be to scold
but to call them, with exuberance, to breakfast.

UNDERSONG

Between dawn and dusk the weather changes,
mountain waters shot through with clear light,
a clear light that makes men joyful:
the wanderer, lulled, forgets to go home.

So begins a poem from the fifth century by Hsieh Ling yun.
So let go, ease away, follow the line of sight out the small
window to the great vehicle.
                              Within twenty yards
of the house, fifteen deer. Three bedded in the sun, twelve
feeding on what grows at the base of dead weeds and grass.
Relaxed but alert, poised, precise in the way they lift each hoof,
raise and lower their muzzles to browse, lick each other's fur,
scratch a flank. Now between two a brief sparring, a feint, a kick,
a leap, and back to browsing.
                              One hunches slightly
and drops her steaming pellets on the snow; another, supple
as a willow, licks the white fur under her own tail. And notice
the ears, all those ears still or in motion, the lovely long ears,
open doors in the air.
                              Whistler Pond is frozen. The turtles
must be deep in mud asleep. Deer trails lead from shore to shore.

With a sound like a rusty hinge worked fast a cock pheasant bursts
into flight at the side of the road.
                              A train horn blows
across the marsh. Twelve carloads of blackened ponderosa pines
headed for some mill—and there we are sitting on the porch last summer,
late at night, watching fire race up the ridge above Blodgett Canyon,
astonished at the height and speed of the flames, and there are the elk
standing in red and gold, knee deep in the east fork, holding to calm
beneath the conflagration.
                              It doesn't hurt to bow to flames
latent in the wood, to honor the elk's strong heart.

                                                            Sound
of a small plane fades to the east, footsteps on crunchy snow slow
then stop. A bald eagle cries a yellow spark above the river,

thrusts out his long feathered legs, back-sweeps his broad wings,
lands in the top branches of a bare tree next to his mate and big
scruffy offspring.
                        Three sets of hungry eyes, make it four,
white clouds, patches of blue above the snow-sleek ridges
of the Bitterroot, and below and in the midst the god we pray to,

water spreading calm beneath the banks, flashing, braiding
through roots and stones, funneling in waves and riffles into runs
long and stroking or short, quick jubilations of water with power

to unclench, unknot, soothe.
                        So let go. Slip out over the water
like a kingfisher, skim the snow downstream to coral clouds
of winter willow, smoky lines of cottonwood above cut-banks

where the river sweeps, glides, and hums a constant undersong.

STEPS

Clouds look small in the distance
as they drift off the sharp peaks
of the southern Bitterroot and move east
almost imperceptibly changing shape—
a mouse becomes an otter,
a squirrel stretches into a greyhound,
the head of a bird separates
                              from its feathery shoulders,
and the soft white body of Spain
drifting a moment ago over the Sapphires
breaks now into islands.
                              Step down
out of the menagerie of clouds,
out of the slow sweep and drift of this spring sky
to the burned forest. There is a ridge I know
at the edge of the burn where the elk path
is still visible in the ash. Green shoots
light up the cinders as clouds pass.

At dusk the mushroom pickers
in blackened clothes head down the mountain.
Elk listen, and when the scent of men
begins to fade they rise from their beds
and step down into the burned meadows.

Half moon lights the valley,
the slopes, and this dirt road
where little pools of shadow show
in the tracks of hooves and boots.
                              The buck veers off,
the woman and her dog keep walking,
a regular cadence, heel & toe, pad & claw.

A bat works a hatch, soft-flapping

in wide circles before the moon
hanging over the meadow
                              up One Horse Creek
where the Indian woman, her neighbor,
broke the pall of grief, ran shouting

and jumping barefoot over rocks
flinging handfuls of Cathy's ashes
in the air, fell down, came back sweating, smiling,
ashes on her face and hands.

Sweet, fast-talking Cathy. Friend.
Friend to all dogs. Who went to the doctor on Thursday
and was dead Sunday.

Ashen moonlight over the meadow, shape-changing.
At the end of the road a dog barks.

THE LIVING HAIR OF TRAVELERS

Smoke from the three stacks
on the outskirts of Salt Lake
yellows the snow on the mountains.
I see patches of green grass
along the runway and beads of rain
on the window of the plane
streaking away like comets
as the Big L1011 lifts off
sucking in the clouds, cutting through the weather.

Here, one can be a connoisseur of hair,
all those heads, above or sinking down
or lulling to one side or the other
along the seat tops—frost, grease, down,
snow, waves, kinks, thatch and curls—
midnight, noon, just after sunset,
afternoon glare—hair or no hair.

They are sleeping. They are reading
about the Unabomber, the teenagers
lying wounded or dead
or running through the streets of Monrovia
in Nikes with assault weapons.
They are reading *Sky* and *People*.

Here in the collective roar
of the expiring century there is an odd comfort
in this anonymous being together
I want to remember.
Look—bald heads lit by reading lights,
and the living hair of travelers
speeding through the clouds.

DRIVING THROUGH

Lolo, Montana

Over time Triple T truck stop turned into Two Bears Sinclair turned into Lucky Diamond Casino and Exxon. Sometimes I stop for gas. Sometimes I notice things, see something memorable. Once, stopped at the light, I watched five deer run across the school yard past the swings and leap one by one over the chain-link fence and clatter across the asphalt of the intersection just before the light changed. What timing, what grace, as they ran, white flags flying, past the Conoco station and the IGA. Another time rounding the bend in the highway just north of Lolo, an icy winter morning on the way to work, saw two deer out of the corner of my eye running down the mountain, the steep cut above the highway. A white pickup in front of me going about fifty, picking up speed, didn't see the deer until too late. The first one made it across, the second was cut completely in half—a burst of steam, sudden release of body heat, spirit made visible hung in the cold air an instant before it too was torn. Sometimes I am so lost in my thoughts I hardly notice Lolo. One day, dreaming of Basho in the Bitterroot, thinking of his haiku

> *Ice tastes bitter*
> *in the mouth of the sewer rat*
> *quenching his thirst*

how the poem seemed clear to me, how the scholar explicating the poem seemed to miss the point. There is a reference, the scholar explained, to a passage in the Chuang-Tzu, a Taoist classic, which says that a sewer rat's thirst is easily quenched with a tiny drink from a large river, and so on. I thought, where would this sewer rat find ice? Why wouldn't it taste bitter? How does one become a sewer rat anyway, if not for some grave failure in this life or another? And there was a hitch-hiker with a pack on his back, a sparse beard, dark weather-worn skin, bright eyes, indeterminate age—a young man

35

who looked old? An old man who looked young? He could have been Basho wandering the western paradise on his journey to the interior. He could have been Chief Looking Glass back to see what we were doing to the sacred land. I drove right through his questioning stare. Then the only light for thirty miles turned red. The time and temperature did a digital shuffle on the Savings & Loan sign. I started to feel like a sewer rat on my way to another meeting with my colleagues to vote on someone's fate. I turned around right there and went back for Basho, for Chief Looking Glass, for the one walking through Lolo.

LIKENESS

Wearing our psychic costumes,
gorilla suits, rhinestone capes, hornet's-nest
masks of affliction, we seem to be lost,

dazed, almost defeated, squeezed
between pleasure and danger, the lub-dub
in the metaphorical heart of the country.

Like shoppers with time running out
and leaden credit cards we move
through the rows, anonymous, feeling

that presence the name-brand garments,
hanging in stillness, have crossed borders
and oceans to grace, and thereby earn

a kind of citizenship one plantigrade step
past the insane, illusionary, yet no less real,
nets and snares of commerce.

We don't plan to wring blood from the sleeves
or spoil the silk with tears.
We want a style to charm, to free us

from so much death and decline.
We want to look in the mirror
without seeing the past and the present

cancel us out. We want to see
the real animal, not necessarily the Rilkean
deer who would bow and drink

from the eternal pool, but the alert one
startled, moved by the likeness
of the other.

ELEGY FOR BIG RED

You were a bastard hatched
in Nebraska, shipped to Montana
in a box with dozens of others
wide-eyed in yellow fluff. Boxes stacked
six feet high in the feed store
filled with a motherless peeping din.
We bought two sacks of feed
and got you and nine others for free,
took you home and raised you
in a bigger box in the basement,
changing your water and feed and newspapers
you soiled and slept on and walked on
for weeks, pecking at the black letters,
thriving it seemed in the light
and warmth of a bare bulb. Soon
you were a little taller than the others
and we knew we'd get no eggs from you.
Through the seasons your constant concern
was your harem of hens. You'd dance
on one leg, shimmy a wing, distract a hen
with the brilliance of your feathers
then grab her neck in your beak
and mount her quickly. Sometimes,
merely at your approach, the hens
would squat down and lift their tails,
sometimes they'd run away squawking
in protest. You followed them everywhere,
standing tall and vigilant, ever protective
of the flock, warding off anything or anyone,
crowing at all hours of the day. Once
the neighbor's golden retriever carried you off
in his teeth when you threw yourself
between the hens and his charge. It took
months to re-grow those long looping

tail feathers that shimmered and bounced
when you strutted, and you strutted
everywhere. I fed and watered you
with a stick in my hand to ward you off.
Over and over you attacked my legs,
from the side or from behind or straight on,
throwing yourself with all your might,
spearing with those sharp yellow horn-hard
three-inch spurs. You drew blood
through my blue jeans. I have scars on both legs
from your fierce attacks. More than once
in anger I punted you like a football across the yard.
My booted foot broke the spur from your left leg.
You learned to lead with your right.
You attacked my sons and their friends,
you took the fun out of raising chickens.
Still, for a couple of sweet years you strutted
among the healthy hens who laid more eggs
than we could eat. Every morning at dawn
you greeted the sun, or, more likely, challenged it.
Every minute of every day you stood
between the hens and all the world's dangers:
dogs, cats, foxes, ravens, hawks, owls, weasels,
and us humans who put up with your bad behavior
and cared for you like one of the family.
One by one over the years the hens died off
or were snatched by predators. We ate the eggs
we didn't sell, then there weren't enough to sell,
then there weren't enough to eat. One of the last
hens, a blue Auracana, broody and determined,
hatched two chicks, red like you. They are still
alive. At dawn I heard an eerie silence
I didn't recognize, and when I went to do
my chores I found you headless in the chicken yard,
red feathers strewn in a path from your perch,
making it clear whatever predator killed you
had to catch you sleeping to do it. I miss you

as I never thought I would. Yesterday
you were this big red fearless strutting rooster
in bright glistening feathers crowing wild at the sun,
and today you are a silent headless corpse.

READING MONTANA

On the road from Dillon to Missoula
just outside of Deerlodge I stop
to walk along the Clark Fork.
Reed-canary grass and red willows
waving in the wind, the wind
blowing wisps of snow off the high ridge

of Deerlodge Mountain, blue-smudged clouds
drifting south as the clouded waters
flow north. Acres of logs in the stack yard
across the river, engines of the mill humming
under the wind. The water tower and red bricks
of the old Montana prison catch the winter sun,

and a rusting motor with weeds
growing out of the manifold
rests among rocks in the river.
A pair of mallards dabble along the banks
above a creek-mouth where a beaver dam
glints with ice and falling water.

The iridescent head of the drake
flashes like a jewel. I walk under the girders
of the bridge over the Clark Fork
where swallows have made nests of mud
and someone, in a clear hand, has written
What have you done to the earth?

What have you done to our fair sister?
The Burlington Northern howls by,
boxcars bright with graffiti, heading south
toward Opportunity, just down the road
from Anaconda, a great burial site
for dredged heavy-metal toxic soil,

accumulated waste from a century
of copper mining, moved downstream
by the pure force of the river.
They've finally removed, such a gentle
word for it, the Milltown dam. Now
they are bull-dozing and scoop-loading
the toxic ground onto trains, or

trucking it back closer to the old mines,
those scars left to fester and drain
into the river's future. But the people
who live in Opportunity wonder
why their place has been designated

a sacrifice zone, why their rugs
were chosen to sweep the dust under.
Upstream Warm Springs Creek
looks pristine as it rushes down
its newly sculpted course. And fish,
they say, are thriving. Sunlight

shines down through the stream
lighting those water-smoothed rocks
from the basement of time that seem
to speak to those who listen.
And water doesn't lie, though, like the wind,
it can keep a secret. In beauty and damage

we walk, reading Montana,
what we have written and what we have not.

LUNCH IN LIMA

Occasionally a traveler may ask, "What's it like
to live in Lima, Montana?" And the answer comes
in the form of an old joke, "Ten months of winter
and two months of company." All along the bar
the citizens bow before their beers or coffees
and give thanks to Social Security, while the poker
machine in the corner goes ping and pays out
another hand with a one-eyed Jack and a pair
of fives. There are faces in Lima
that look like the land. The land around Lima
is mountains and pastures, pastures that resemble
chess boards, cows for pawns, horses for knights,
a bishop on a backhoe, a bishop on a four-wheeler.
The queen is a hawk on a fence post, the king
is the board itself in checkmate to the land.
The sky is truly big, but also heavy or light or
furiously out of focus in blowing snow.
Most hopes are kept small to fit in the pockets
of overalls. The wind, the wind is the wind
blowing a plastic bag, a wolf's howl, a rooster's
cry, a human sigh, dreams of antelope and cattle,
exhaust of trucks, and smoke from all the chimneys
in Lima, translating everything into its own
ancient tongue. But step in, close the door
on the wind. Today's special at Jan's Café
is an Indian Taco, fry bread smothered with chili,
cheese, lettuce, onion and tomato. Jan herself
will smile and offer free refills as long as lunch
lasts, and then it's goodbye Jan, goodbye Lima,
and back out into the wind.

THE SPELL OF THE BITTERROOT

Our river runs north, map-wise anyway,
but it has been ditched and diked,
riprapped and rerouted,
dredged and diverted,
channelized, head-gated, and privatized
in many places. Portages abound,
and no-trespassing signs hang from strands
of barb-wire strung across braids.
This is not right.
But does the river care? It just wants
to meander, take its own sweet time,
trust in gravity and the tidal pull
of eventual dissolution
in the great peace-making sea.
As Vernon Woolsey, our deceased water master
who drifts now in that sea, certainly well knew,
any shoring-up or riprapping the banks
will have consequences downstream.
Sometimes it seems history
is simply a string of bad ideas,
like lining the banks of the river
with wrecked cars.
A pristine trout stream
sandwiched between two lanes
of the stalled traffic of the dead.
But then fenders, hoods, and mangled grills
broke loose from the cables,
batteries wept acid over the stones,
headlights and windshields ground
into a kind of sand, and the sleek coupes
and sedans of lost decades
littered the bars and beaches.
Progenitor of the caddis and stonefly,
the midge and the trout, our river

runs under the spell of anastomosis;
from the Greek for opening,
ana, throughout, and *stoma,* mouth;
a mouth that won't stay closed,
a network of living vessels, veins
in a watery leaf of earth,
channels, braids, a continuous flow
of wild water. Just as we do,
our river wants to stretch out
and move freely in its own bed.

RAIN ON THE RIVER

The river is high and clouded, little
by little cutting the east banks,
washing soil from among the roots.
Big pines and cottonwoods falling to snags

forming pockets, temporary cover,
holding water for trout. Water says
everything's temporary, everything's moving,
trees, gravel bars, the new house

where the roofer kneels, nailing shingles
in light rain. Look, water says,
right now, before and after—
raindrops falling into clouds on the sunlit river.

III

LOWER YELLOWSTONE FALLS

Standing on asphalt laid down on rock
just at the place where the Yellowstone River
has come around a bend, riffling,
picking up speed, hugging a big rock
cutting the current, island-like,
just before the river forms
a last slick run to a ledge of rock,

a brief horizon,

and falls down the cliff face
into the chasm of the lower canyon
in a continuous roar
a whitewater storm hosannaing hard
down through layers of air
watery columns collapsing
waves breaking into shafts
shafts breaking into tumbling ovoid
shapes pulling apart
colliding in a rush the eye
can't stop or hold
so the body feels its falling
as uprush through legs hips
into the solar plexus the heart
the blasting synapses
sheathed in water—Step back.
Hold on.
                A golden stonefly
lifts off the lip of the falls,
hovers like a spark in the mist.

RATTLESNAKE BEND

Leave the gold in the ore, leave the water in the river,
leave the rattlesnakes alone.

This is the Smith River so there are white cliffs and white
pelicans with black-tipped wings, swallows that dart and glide
tracing intricate patterns and arcs through air
over the water,

meadows of horse mint, hare bells, sunflowers, and lupine,
the green invader, leafy spurge, and the spiked crowns
of purple thistle.

The sky is deepest blue over one cliff, and over another
cliffs of cloud are building to a storm. Rock doves
coo from a ledge above Rattlesnake Bend

as one after another three rafts full of people bounce down
through the rapids, disembark on the beach. This
is the good time of summer they've come for.

Sons and daughters, mothers and fathers, brothers and sisters,
friends and cousins, and one good yellow dog, arrived
at Camp Rattlesnake in rivertime

and wouldn't you know it, little Liza steps over one
on the trail to the privy. Her brother Sam hollers *Snake!*
to save the day and his sister.

The men and women drop the gear they're hauling
and swing into action. One father fashions a forked stick,
another picks up a large rock, and soon everyone is marveling

at the writhing headless body of the snake. The boys pick it up,
wrestle the still-living muscle in their hands.

Everyone stands around in a loose circle as the sun goes down
watching as the body begins to relax. Now what, no one says.

One of the fathers has a thought, and this thought is shared
by others: let's not waste this life we've taken.
"Let's cook it and eat it," he says.

Later, everyone tucked away in tents, the snake is there
in the sound of the river.

EVENING LANDSCAPE

The smallest of bugs
falls from my apple tree in Montana

onto the Japanese landscape print,
ambles across a mountain,

steps onto a maple leaf,
then walks off into sky

toward the distant geese.
It is a woodblock print by Hiroshige,

maple leaves and branches
framing a view of Tekona Shrine

at Mama, ten miles east
of old Edo, now Tokyo. Late sun

lights the lake where, according
to legend, the beautiful maiden,

Tekona, drowned herself
to escape the rivalries of too many suitors.

A blush of sunset rises over
the mountains and shines on the water

as the small bug steps off the page
into evening air.

NOTES FOR A PAINTING

for Jim Galvin

Smoke rises gray-blue,
　　　　　　　　almost screening
a line of sprinklers working in circles
　　　　　　　　　　　　to green the pasture
bordered on the west by a dirt road bordered
　　　　　　　　　　　　by telephone lines.
A dark stand of ponderosas, elder spirits,
　　　　　　　　　　　hold to the north hills.
Where dark works its way toward the horizon
　　　　　　　　　　　a poor farmstead,
gray-boarded barn, holes
　　　　　　in the roof,
　　　　　　　　leans tiredly toward the mountains and
a graveyard of old cars, one
　　　　　　　　　　　like a turquoise stone
　　　　　　　　　　　set in a bone bracelet.
To the south a yellow slope rises and falls, tinted
　　　　　　　　　　　with faint patches
of lavender,
　　　　rises and falls and rises again toward a distant soft line of
mountains
　　　　　　turning into weightless mountains
　　　　　　　　　　　of cloud
or clouds of smoke—
In the foreground
　　　　　　either a fence post without rails
　　　　　　　　　where a robin looks out,
or a wheelless rusted robin-colored truck
　　　　　　　　　in window-high weeds,
or, one black horse, head down, oblivious.

53

AFTER THE FIREWORKS

Last night's fireworks still sparking
on retinas, blister on my ring-finger
where Amelia's sparkler touched me
with its magic. Summer's showering,
rolling, trotting off across the pasture
like a herd of calves startled by the celebration.
Morning after under a drifting, calving shelf
of clouds. A tiger swallowtail visits the purple
bird vetch. Sparks in gray daylight.
Migrant mushroom pickers work the high burns
of the Bitterroot. Gone are the golden morels
of the river bottom, fast-going the blacks
on the slopes, the bigger grays coming on.
First cutting of hay has farmers wishing off rain
they prayed for. Crack of hammers and leftover
firecrackers sound over the drone of mowers.
Time and timing, work and weather wheeling.
In Amelia's eyes mountains float.

ETHERIDGE

In his tiger-tooth necklace, his striped shirt,
and black-rimmed glasses, he sits
in the judge's chair. He tells us how he died

in Korea from a shrapnel wound
and was resurrected by dope, how he died again
in prison and was brought back to life

by the poem. He tells us how the faces
of his family helped him see through stone,
how, even though the voice may be strident

or angry, the poem comes from love.
He tells us about feeling fucked up.
He laughs. He makes the sound

of the drum, *kah doom/ kah doom-doom*
kah doom/ kah doom-doom-doom
He sings *Willow, Weep for Me*, for us.

He throws his head back,
closes his eyes and sings.
When he bends down into a poem

in this courtroom where the murder trial
has been postponed he closes his eyes
and we can hear frogs and crickets

along a Mississippi roadside
and look up through the dark
at stars blinking in hell.

ELEGY FOR JIM WELCH

Over the treetops, a big empty blue.

A mourning dove calls, *where are you*

Twin whitetail fawns lie in the shade
of cottonwoods near the irrigation ditch
we crossed, a little drunk, one dark winter
night years ago, your hands on my shoulders,
Lois' hands on yours—the blind leading the blind,
someone said, all of us laughing.

Now a young fox, light August red, stops
at the edge of shade and holds unmoving
as though posed mid-stride by a taxidermist,
except for the eyes which shift their focus
through dappled light of the hawthorn thicket
with a fierce precision, and except for the black
nostrils that sample and sort the layered scents
of morning air—faint musk of deer droppings,
dusty fluff from a finch's abandoned nest,
the nitrogen aura of decaying duff above
interlaced roots of pine and wild pear,
scent-sparks of shell-chips left by the pheasant's
hatchlings, and traces of human presence
still pooling in footprints.

The dove calls, *where are you, you you*

Out beyond the blue, stars wait to fall.

The fox, a long pause between breaths,
stands poised on three legs in the sun,

then, like a gust of red wind, turns
through the leaves and is gone.

BIG LOST RIVER BREAKDOWN

The truck broke down at Craters of the Moon.
We sit in the asphalt parking lot
paved over the lava, our trip to California
stopped like the flow under the big open
sky of Idaho. A bird snatches a black butterfly
out of the air. Clouds move like a slow caravan
on the southern horizon. Hours pass,
going nowhere. The last volcanic cinders
cool for a thousand years.

In the wrecker headed east to Arco
King Mountain at the south end
of the Lost River Range slowly rises
in the windshield. Closer
we can see the numbered years
painted in white on the face of a cliff,
each in a different hand. Stan,
the young driver, explains the tradition.
Each year a group from the senior class
hikes up the mountain with ropes
then hangs a volunteer down over the cliff
in an old tire to paint their graduation year.
What may look like defacement to a traveler
is a point of pride for the graduates of Arco High.

Arco, Idaho, the first town in the free world
to be lit by the split atom, ten years after
Hiroshima and Nagasaki. July 17, 1955.
Deep as the Grand Canyon this human urge
to stop time, to be free of its burden and shadow.
Atoms for Peace, says the sign in the park
across the road from Grandpa's Southern Bar B-Q.
Sunflowers along the roadside bow
to passing cars.

Days pass, going nowhere. Good ribs
slow-cooked on a split-barrel stove
under the cottonwoods, the smoke
sweetening the summer air dawn to dusk
makes us recall Dreamland

in Jerusalem Heights outside Tuscaloosa,
white bread, slabs and red sauce, beer
in a can, NO DANCIN NO CUSSIN
said the sign on the wall. And Archibald's
drive-in barbecue, the blackened smoker hole
in a pink brick wall, white Styrofoam cups
of magic sauce, Northport, Alabama, and
that place just off Speedway in Tucson
with the signed black-and-white photos
of movie stars on the wall.

Whatever else happens in this mangled world,
Grandpa says, the good cookin goes on.
Everybody know got to feed both body and soul.
Grandpa came out from Kentucky, can't remember
the story, maybe with the military, maybe
his truck broke down in Arco. Weeks passed,
going nowhere. Then the smell of those ribs
cooking cast a spell over the neighborhood,
drifted up the highway past the city limit sign,
enough to make a hungry person sigh.

The radio sitting on the window sill
tells us a visitor from Sydney, Australia
was gored by a bison at Old Faithful Geyser,
and a young man beaten and left for dead
in a creek runs away from the hospital
at 4 A.M. and a month later calls the sheriff
to report what happened. Arrest warrants
have been issued. There was a fire
in a grain elevator, and the drought continues.

This afternoon at one o'clock, in Arco Atomic
Auditorium, the big lava rock building on
Main Street, the doors will open for
the Annual Quilt Show. Admission is free,
donations accepted, and there will be a raffle.

The quilts say peace and bless this home,
the log cabins, the wedding rings, the flowering
fields, the wild goose chase patterns stitched
by hand as the hours pass. Down the street
heat waves rise from a gray metal building,
Lost River Ballistic Technologies.

And at the Lost River Motel they boast
"the best plot of grass in Arco." A place
to sit and watch the sparse traffic
on Highway 93, listen to cicadas buzzing
in the brush, sparrows cheeping
in the Chinaberry tree.

Across the road a giant green rocking chair
in front of Pickle's Place, a photo op,
so anyone who climbs up and sits in it
will look like a small child.
In the parking lot a brown dog,
who looks like she's been dumped,
watches every car that passes
from her patch of shade beneath the sign.
A car pulls in, she trots up anxiously,
looking for her master, runs alongside
until the car stops and the door opens.
She sniffs the air, then turns in disappointment
and goes back to her spot to wait
like a good dog.

The hours pass, going nowhere.
And we wait. Who knows when

we'll hit the road again? The real moon
rises over Craters of the Moon
and the black sprawl of its lava flows.
Somewhere near Arco
the Big Lost River goes underground.
On the face of King Mountain
the years pass and someone paints them.

RED MOON

August sky cloudless, smokeless,
a high deep blue that softens
and fades toward the horizon
where the sleepless mountains float
like overloaded barges in a mist.

A pale yellow mayfly lands
on the back of my hand—translucent wings
upheld, set like a sail tacking
in the breeze, turns its whole small
body to return my gaze. Orb eyes
consider me before it lifts off,
vanishes into air. Light touch, brief affair.

The river runs black with ash
and mud, two days of rain
through last summer's burned slopes,
choking the gravel bars, cutting off light
in the water so shade that made
the depths complex lies on the surface.
Dark days for the fish.

Dark days. Fires burned so hot streams
boiled. A stallion reared and battered
against fence rails. Yellow-shirted men
and women worked for weeks in ash
and cinders. Smoke choked the valley.
One day in town we stepped out of a store
at four in the afternoon, smoke so thick
and dark lights in the parking lot had come on.

Fires gone, the mountains bleed.

Now the first white cloud pushes up,

a tentative thought, from the western ridge,
rises into the wide blue.

Make a contrary motion, Miles said.
Put a streak of red up against the blue.
Light a backfire in memory, but keep moving.
Full moon, red moon. She's come and gone.

She left hours ago. And the man
waking alone in a dark room
remembers her motion, his own,
slow, then wild, then subsiding
into a lingering scent of almonds and ash.

LUMINOUS HOUR

Dragonflies, bees, grasshoppers
rev their engines in the late afternoon.
Water in the ditch falls over
the rock dam the children built years ago.
Water has a certain sound as it passes
beneath the cottonwoods, a different sound
as it passes beneath pines, and slows near the dam.
Down the Bitterroot range the ridge lines
form a scale of colors, six or seven shades
of blue-gray. The mountains wear shifting
veils of light. It is the hour the crickets
in the draw begin. Wings of midges
fly in luminous patterns around lit globes
of milkweed, not like the stark and starving
planets orbiting the sun, but electrons
bounding through a quickened pulse, sparks
flying from some good idea ignited in the blood.

WHERE SUNLIGHT FALLS

Her body is a free country
bordered by infinite space.

Here in the shadows of the apple tree
where sunlight falls on yellow paper,

a land of shimmering lakes
and quiet ponds she gazes down on,

it's all here, she thinks,
in the mind's leaves and scarred branches.

She thinks, *Life is hard,* and fragile,
and sweet, and trouble.

She's leaning into a kiss,
she's slipping out of her slip,

she's feeling the sudden glow
of a sunset breaking through clouds

over the stands. The count is 0 and two,
bases loaded, two outs.

Her man-sized son cocks
his bat, eyes the pitch, swings—

She hears the ping, makes a wish,
follows the small, hard, stitched world

out into the generous space
beyond the fence.

LAR & DEER

On the porch at Wawona he would sit
in his wheelchair and watch the deer.

He spoke with his clear eyes
and his palsied body.

Did you see Ginger today? Ginger was a doe.
Yes, he said, by looking right at you

and raising his eyebrows and stiffening his back.
Do you want to go inside now?

No, he said, pursing his lips and lowering his eyes.
For thirty years he was fed with a spoon

and a spill-proof cup. Sometimes he would choke
and spit up like an infant.

When he had to go, someone had to go with him
and hold him on the toilet and wipe him clean.

Sometimes he would sigh and smile the calmest smile.
When he was happy and excited he would kick his feet

and wave his arms like broken flowers.
The deer came right up to him

and ate the grain scattered at his feet
and sniffed his knees
and breathed with him in the early evening.

IV

THAT SPACE INSIDE THEM

There is a space up in the air
where the hundred and seventh floor was,

where Rosy and her lover
sit waiting at a small table with wine glasses

and white napkins folded like flowers.
They sip the wine and look into each other's

eyes, and it is as if no one else is there.
Two glasses of red wine, two of ice water,

two eager young bodies dressed for the evening,
two pairs of lips saying words they won't remember.

Somewhat shy and momentarily at a loss,
they hold hands across the table, gaze

out the windows at black water
rimmed with lights. Two tugs and two barges

barely moving, and down below
on her little island, dressed

in green lights, Liberty looks small,
vulnerable, a charm on a bracelet.

Now, and years from now
they will hold that space inside them,

their own faces reflected in the glass
they look through into lighted distances,

and they will hold that image of tender
Liberty against the other.

DEER IN THE GARDEN

for Coleman

He started up the old Ford pickup
and drove slowly out the dirt and gravel road
past the fenced garden where a young whitetail deer
was browsing withered vines in the fall sun.
As the truck went by, the deer startled
and began throwing itself at the fence,
although the gate across the way was open.
He watched in the rearview mirror
as the deer threw itself again and again
against the fence, ramming with head
and shoulder, confused, terrified, pitting
all its strength against the wire fence.
It was too much. He stopped the truck
and ran back to the garden, through the gate,
and, abandoned to his task, in a series
of quick moves, threw his arms around
the wild deer, lifted and turned it in the air,
as their wide eyes met, then heaved it
toward the gate. He drew a deep breath
and stared as the deer leapt free
and bounded off across the grass, its white
tail pointed straight up at the sky.

HARVEST HOME

A bright terrain of river stones,
gravel, and sand, wild purple asters
nodding in a breeze, goldenrod, stunted willows,
knapweed, and five kinds of grass
form the landscape of this island
in the Lochsa River where I sit on a drift log
picking through recent memory—

my two boys eating those big sugary
pastries called elephant ears
at the Ravalli county fair, seeing emu,
python, the shy fallow deer, pushy goats
and piglets at the petting zoo, walking
through the produce barn admiring the man
made of zucchini, melon belly, cabbage
head, peapod mouth, radish eyes.
The boys both touching winter squash,
comparing pumpkins. And down
the midway, how they observed carefully

the carnival rides: the Kamikaze,
Zipper, Yoyo, the Gravitron, gauging
their fear against possible joy.
And finally the giant strawberry
they chose to sit inside
and spin a wheel that spun the berry
in quick circles within circles in the sun.

PRAISE

for Clay

Coming home from a day on the river
I find my eleven-year-old son cutting down
cottonwood trees. What's up? I ask.
I'm building a cabin, he tells me.
And I think how this instinct to build
is caught up in the need to tear down.
Witness the last vestiges of the great
American forests. I know, I know.
Rilke said, "for only in praising
is my heart still mine, so violently
do I know the world." We need to know
our hearts apart from the violent world.
I would rather praise than complain.
Praise my son, the woodcutter, the builder.
Praise the fall sun glinting on the river.
Praise the clear water where the cutthroat
and rainbow spawn on the same gravel.
Praise the young woman lying naked
in the sun beside the river at Bell Crossing.
May the sun turn away before she burns.
And if I must complain may it not be
from boredom or bitterness or the nervous
need to define the self in opposition
to something, but let my complaints rise
selectively, as wild trout rise,
from the waters of praise.

VIEW OF THE BITTERROOT

Way out on gold slopes
of the wheat field,
once shoals of an ancient
glacial lake, three deer
wade shoulder-deep in wheat
and seem to float
like leaf boats on a gold stream.

A dark stand of Ponderosa pine
backs the scene, still spires
brushed and dabbed with morning sun.
And past the pines
the mountains build in steel-blue waves
to saw-tooth ridges in the sky.

The new owners of the wheat field
plan to develop the land, cut
the acres, where the sandhill cranes
return each year, down into small lots,
five hundred houses packed in tight
like gold bars in rows
over the shallow aquifer
at the edge of the marsh.

A GOLD STAR FOR CRUMLEY

On the wall behind the bar, black and white
photos of those who told stories, drank Irish,
Scotch, bourbon on the rocks, or beer
with a little tomato juice and salt.
Why the gold stars? *You get those when you die,*
you explained. *Relax. What'll you have to drink?*
This is my friend Earl. We call him The Duke.
He did two tours in Viet Nam, and one
in Deerlodge. He's here most nights.
And you laughed, Jim, after half the things you said.
I can still hear you laughing, wise-cracking,
code-talking, listening with care, and telling
small stories against the big back-drop
outside the windows. Your corner stool
at The Depot will support a heavy emptiness
no matter how light the moment, no matter
how true the story. Now who will declare
the last good kiss? Who will dance with the bear?
Each dawn the sun in the window, when it comes,
will be your gold star.

ELEGY FOR THE YANGTZE

Up in the clouds the illustrious dead fish for us.

—Bei Dao

Now the engineers of disaster drown the river
that inspired ten thousand poems.
They've halted the flow of the great Yangtze
and soon the rapids roaring through the gorges
since before the time of man
will fall silent, choked off, silted in.
The immortals fly back and forth
above the rising water
as perches they've used for centuries
go under. Over a million people
forced to leave their homes,
two cities, eleven large towns,
one thousand three hundred fifty two villages
soon to disappear beneath the muddy water.
The numbers like belts cinched tight
around the earth. Li Peng,
who ordered the tanks to crush the students
in Tiananmen Square, ordered the river
to stop. His legacy: tried to stop the flow
of earth's chi, to x-out the yin and the yang.
But it's too late for blame.
The oracle bones dissolve in mud.

DOG

Come back, his master calls, breathless to the dog.
The wind blows his voice away, away goes the dog.

I have tried in dreams to find you,
Conjured your touch, your scent, wandering like a lost dog.

They carried away what they could as the waters rose.
No room in the truck for the dog.

Bogalusa to Baghdad, Juarez to Jerusalem,
Who feeds the nameless dog?

God is great god is small
Open the envelope, pet the dog.

GOOD NIGHT IRENE

The bullet hole in six-inch-thick plexiglass,
though chilling, had a kind of glacial beauty
all its own—aqua light suffused through ice.

The black face of the night nurse,
though she had seen it all,
still shone with a hint of warmth
for a stranger come to visit his mother.

Palm leaves rattled in a warm breeze
off the Pacific, fluorescent lights buzzed
and sputtered outside the hospital, gunshots
snapped in the distance, sirens wailed
through intersections along the grid:
Anaheim & Cedar, Ninth & Pine,
Blood & Bone, Almost & Not Yet.

Erma, her friend, had called to say
the operation went well. She was recovering
when she had a stroke.

In this photo, black & white, *Flat tire,*
Eel River, 1947, she squints in the sun,
leans over as if she is trying to duck the snapshot,
as if she is saying, *Jeez, Larry,*
stop clowning and get this spare on.
My infant face looks over her shoulder.

Seven smiling women standing in the grass
on Juanita Street under phone wires,
feathery fronds of the Mexican fan palm,
and gray sky that must have been blue.
High heels, belted dresses, rhinestones,
and pearls: The Peters Girls: Jimmie, Irene,

Ruth, Ruby, Millie, Jewel, and Wanda (Jinx).
Jimmie, the youngest, holds a cigarette
between her fingers, the ash about to fall
into the geraniums blooming at her ankles.
Beautiful Irene and her sisters, born
in an Appalachian coal town, migrated west.
This photo doesn't say what brought them all together.

I sit beside her bed as she sleeps,
I.V. in her arm, her closed eyes moving,
one side of her mouth slack. I wonder
if she will be able to speak when she wakes.

I think, in the morning, mother, when they
release you into my care, I'll wheel you
along the corridors into the elevators
and out. I'll wheel you out
into the bright Los Angeles sun
and we'll wait for your good friend,
that smiling man from Nigeria, Confidence,
who named his daughter Patience.

IRENE

One hand on her hip and the other
on the hood of a pale blue Buick,
she poses for this happy snapshot
in a Palos Verdes parking lot. Time
is stone that turns to water in her smile.
She loved bright colors, the sheen
of velvet on butterflies' wings.
She dressed in swirls and stripes,
pastels and primaries. She wore
hats that attracted hummingbirds,
and a smile to match the southern
California sun, to ward off gloom
lingering in shadows of all her rooms.
Even in her eighties she put lipstick
kisses on all her letters. She loved
flowers, hibiscus and roses,
chrysanthemums and carnations, poppies
of the desert, redbuds and dogwoods
of Kentucky. As a boy I brought her
bunches of wildflowers, or gladiolas
and irises stolen from Masuda's garden.
And to her last room in Long Beach
I brought an orchid and an amaryllis
that bloomed by her bedside. Time
is water that turns to stone, and the heart
balances emptiness with fullness beat by beat.

CEMETERY IN KENTUCKY

The hours part us
But they bring us
Together again

Old stones with names we know,
plastic flowers faded by the sun,
blown by the wind, this little graveyard
on a hill where moss grows thick
as shag over the buried stories.
Who was Rebecca Soulerette?
Why does the mule standing back
in the trees in dusk hold so still?
Lichen grow among wool curls
on the lamb asleep in stone.
Ice and wind have pitted the cheeks
of the boy cherub kneeling over
the small grave of Freddie Peters.
Under the oak, shadows sway,
a cluster of black umbrellas.
There is some singing in the trees
that comes and goes. Hard truths
the haints rehearse, roots tugging
at their coal-dark hearts, lifting
sighs and mumbled hymns through long
seasons of mud and snow to leaf out
green in sun along the limbs.
A scarlet tanager haunts these leaves
with fleeting joy, and a bobcat
slinks along the dirt track below
the power lines down the hill
sniffing for scent of its lost mate.
Roots of the oak form a seat
where one can sit and read
the stone words at the angel's feet:

Mothers plant the seeds of love
That bloom forever. Fathers help some.
Budd Ball's stone says he fought
and died in the Spanish-American War.
The angel cast in concrete cradles
a bird's nest like an infant
in her arms, hope's best tableau,
and her long hair and long dress
flow in a perpetual light breeze.
Her great, feathered wings look
as though they could lift her.
Sweet mother, forgive the fire,
we brought your ashes home.

WHITE CHURCH IN WIBORG

When I first peered through the window of the white church
on the hill in Wiborg I saw, with the help of family stories
and old photographs, my great grandfather, the Reverend
James Fletcher Peters standing in his black coat and long
gray beard with his hands held out before him
as though he were holding an invisible gift,

and offering it to those sitting attentively in their best clothes
in those long hardwood body-worn and polished pews.
What he held in his eyes and hands, I thought I knew,
and wanted to say. Jim was there, and Ada, and all
their children, the dead and the living. Laurence sat
next to Ralph, his younger brother, who he shot and killed

with Jim's shotgun, accidentally, one mild spring afternoon
in the room where their sisters Ruby, Ruth, and the baby
Jewel watched. Ada was pregnant with my mother,
and the terrible grief that dims but never dissolves
must have tattooed the psyche of the still unborn Elsie,
who, eventually, changed her name to Irene.

There were Roberts, Smiths, Thompsons, Vanovers,
Soulerettes, Perrys, and Joneses, and other names
recorded and still legible in old bibles somewhere,
and chiseled into stones leaning like trees
about to fall in the forest that surrounds the small
hilltop graveyard across highway 27.

There was a wagon-rutted mule path that wound
from the church to the baptizing hole that branched off
one way and switch-backed up the hill to the graveyard,
or, if one turned the other way, followed a ridge
through the woods past Beulah Heights and the orphans'
home, Honeybee, and the small drift-mouth mines

that spoke the black tongue of coal
all the way to Cumberland Falls, where one could stand
in the mist on a bright night and watch the Moonbow
rise above the river, like an arched and lighted entrance
through earthly air that made those who saw it lean closer.

NOTES

Page 8: "Ice Fishing in a Snow Storm": The italicized lines are from Liu Tsung-yuan, Tu Fu, and Richard Hugo respectively.

Pages 11, 12 & 13: "Homage to Su Tung-p'o": The italicized lines are from Su Tung-p'o translated by Burton Watson.

Page 34: "Reading Montana": The italicized lines are from *A River Runs Through It* by Norman Maclean.

Page 50: "Red Moon": The italicized line is by Miles Davis.

Page 67: "Cemetery in Kentucky": The italicized lines are from gravestones.